Cambridge Experience Readers

Level 4

Series editor: Nicholas Tims

Tasty Tales

Frank Brennan

CAMBRIDGE
UNIVERSITY PRESS

CAMBRIDGE
UNIVERSITY PRESS

University Printing House, Cambridge CB2 8BS, United Kingdom

One Liberty Plaza, 20th Floor, New York, NY 10006, USA

477 Williamstown Road, Port Melbourne, VIC 3207, Australia

314–321, 3rd Floor, Plot 3, Splendor Forum, Jasola District Centre, New Delhi – 110025, India

103 Penang Road, #05-06/07, Visioncrest Commercial, Singapore 238467

José Abascal 56, 1º – 28003 Madrid, Spain

Cambridge University Press is part of the University of Cambridge.

It furthers the University's mission by disseminating knowledge in the pursuit of
education, learning and research at the highest international levels of excellence.

www.cambridge.org
Information on this title: www.cambridge.org/9788483235423

© Cambridge University Press 2009

First published 2009
Second edition 2015

40 39 38 37 36 35 34 33 32 31 30 29 28 27 26 25

Printed in Spain by Pulmen

Frank Brennan has asserted his right to be identified as the Author of the Work
in accordance with the Copyright, Design and Patents Act 1988.

Illustrations by Kevin Levell (Full English Breakfast, Changes), SaLi (The Water of
Wanting, Kung Fu Spice), Timothy Banks (A Little Pot of Honey, Fugu)

ISBN 978-84-832-3542-3 Paperback; legal deposit: S.939-2009
ISBN 978-84-832-3545-4 Paperback with audio CD/CD-ROM pack for Windows,
Mac and Linux; legal deposit: S.235-2009

No character in this work is based on any person living or dead.
Any resemblance to an actual person or situation is purely accidental.

To P. J. B.

The paper that this book has been printed on is produced using an elemental
chlorine-free (ECF) process at mills registered to ISO14001 (2004), the environmental
management standard. The mills source their wood fibre from sustainably-managed
forests. No hardwood pulp is used in the production of this paper.

Contents

BEFORE YOU READ

• •

1. Look at the cover and the pictures in the book. The stories are about different people and set in different places, but they have a common theme. What do you think it is?

The Water of Wanting

Jean Pascal put a small drop of clear liquid into the drinking water of his mice.

Normally, the mice drank only when they were thirsty. But Jean soon noticed that when there was liquid in the water, they came back to drink it more than usual. They couldn't have been thirsty any more, but they drank. He needed to check this carefully.

Jean was a very careful man.

When he was ten years old, he had tried to relight a firework. He thought the firework was finished, but it wasn't. It was big and expensive and it exploded in his face. Twenty years later he still had the scar on his left cheek where he had been burned by the firework. He was always careful after that.

Jean was now a brilliant chemist. He worked in Montreal, Canada, for a large chemical company. His company made a lot of different chemicals – including chemicals for food, which are often called additives. Additives give food a different colour or flavour or even make it last longer. Food companies pay a lot of money for additives which work well.

* * *

'Sometimes people just don't seem to want to buy something,' Jean's manager, Charles, had told him earlier. 'Companies spend a lot of money on persuading people to buy something, but then nobody wants it.'

'Maybe they don't want it because they don't like it,' Jean had suggested. 'It's their choice, after all.'

'People will like anything if you sell it in the right way,' Charles had said. 'No, we must be missing something out. What can we do to make sure that people will like what we sell? Let's think about that. You're our top chemist, Jean. Can you work on that? Work on something to make people love what they eat and drink!'

That had been a few months ago. Now Jean thought of his manager's words as he looked at his mice.

The mice kept coming back for more water. Their stomachs were already completely full of liquid, but they still wanted to drink more. They just couldn't get enough of the water which had Jean's additive in it. They didn't want to eat any food at all. Soon they died because their tiny bodies were too full of water. And, amazingly, they were still trying to reach the water when they died.

* * *

Jean's son, Alain, was only eighteen months old, but he knew what he didn't like. He didn't like green vegetables. He always threw them away. The green mess on the table had been Alain's vegetable dinner.

Jean smiled as he took Alain from Katya, his wife, and tried to feed the child himself. Katya had given up trying to write her book for a while. She thought she would be able to write while she was at home with their son. But she found she didn't have any time any more. Her eyes were sleepy.

'I can't persuade him to eat any more. I wish I could!' Katya said.

'He eats enough,' Jean said, 'doesn't he?'

'Oh, he's happy to drink milk or eat sugary food,' Katya said. 'But when I try to give him some vegetables, he just shouts and screams!'

Katya was often worried about what their son ate and didn't eat. She had often said she didn't want Alain to eat the unhealthy food people call 'junk food'. Jean and his wife both knew that junk food can make children fat and unhealthy even before they start school. Junk food, like cheap hamburgers and potato fries, usually has too much sugar or salt or other additives in it. The problem is that children often prefer junk food.

'What if,' Jean thought, 'these children could be persuaded to eat healthy food? What if they actually *liked* vegetables?'

*   *   *

Back at work, Jean was still working on his new additive. There was a long chemical name for it, but he preferred to call it 'Water of Wanting' because it made his mice want more. What's more, he rather liked the short name for his additive: *WOW*.

He cut the amount of *WOW* that he added to his mice's water by half. The results were the same. Then he added much smaller amounts of *WOW*: the mice drank less, but they still came back for little drinks of water all the time. These little drinks were still far more than the mice needed. It was as if they had become addicted to water. They weren't interested in anything else. They didn't even want any food. This time they didn't die of too much water. They all died of hunger.

'This,' Jean thought, 'could be a problem.' He wanted *WOW* to help the mice to eat certain food and drink certain drinks. But he didn't want the mice to forget about or ignore[1] all the other things they were given.

Jean had been working extremely hard on this. He hadn't allowed anybody else to help him. *WOW* was his own invention.[2] He had made it all by himself. He wanted people to recognise his work. What's more, he didn't like the thought that somebody else might steal the credit from him. He wanted to be very careful about that.

'How's the work going, Jean?' Charles asked him at the end of one long, difficult day. 'You've been keeping everything to yourself lately. You're our number one chemist, Jean. I like to know what's happening. So, is the work going well?'

'Well, things *are* going well – very well,' Jean told him.

'Hey!' Charles sounded excited. 'Do you mean to say you've found an answer to that problem I mentioned? Because if you have … let me tell you, there'll be a lot of interest in it from a lot of people – a lot of interest!'

'No, Charles,' said Jean. 'I haven't found an answer to the problem, not yet. But I'm a lot closer than I was.'

'A lot closer, you say? That's great!' said Charles. 'OK, we're going to need results soon. Look, I'll have to tell our bosses a bit more about your work – after all, they're paying us to do it; and they're paying us very well. And that means you'll get extra money in your salary if you finish the work. Or perhaps you want more. Is that it, Jean? If you want more, I'm sure it can be arranged – but we need those results …'

Charles didn't need to finish. If Jean's company thought he couldn't complete his work on *WOW*, they would ask somebody else to finish it. Jean didn't want that.

Jean knew he had to tell Charles everything about *WOW* and what it could do. It was the only way to keep the company interested. So he did.

Charles was *very* excited.

'*WOW* sounds amazing!' he cried. 'I'll get some people in to help you and—'

'No!' Jean called out quickly. 'I'm sorry, Charles. I just mean that I'm so close to this that I don't want to go over every step with new people. And I really want to finish it myself. I'm so close, so close.'

'OK, Jean,' Charles said calmly. 'I can understand. But I'm going to have to see some of the work you've done soon. You *do* understand that, don't you?'

'Of course,' Jean said. 'Of course.'

'Great!' Charles replied warmly.

*　*　*

Little Alain's face was red with anger when Jean walked in. He threw his plate of vegetables onto the floor.

Katya was crying.

'I don't know what to do, Jean!' she cried. 'Alain is nearly two years old and I can't get him to eat any healthy food! I have to feed him rubbish because he'd die of hunger if I didn't! I hate this! There must be some way to get him to eat better food! It's making me crazy – I don't know what to do!'

Both Alain and his mother were crying now. Jean hugged his wife and son.

Soon Alain got tired of crying and allowed Jean to feed him some soup while Katya made some coffee.

'I know people say he's going to grow up soon and this problem will stop,' Katya said. 'But what if it doesn't? What if they're wrong?'

* * *

Jean had a lot to do if he was going to make *WOW* work successfully. He wanted *WOW* that would make people want to eat or drink some things but not others. At the same time, he didn't want *WOW* to make people lose control of their appetites.[3]

Jean Pascal was a careful man.

Jean gave his mice a choice of two drinks. One drink had *WOW* in it and the other didn't. The mice still drank from the water with *WOW* in it and left the other drink alone. This time, however, they only drank when they were thirsty. They also ate their food too, just like normal, hungry mice.

At last the *WOW* was successful. Jean looked at his mice and thought hard.

* * *

After some time Jean knocked on the door of Charles's office. He had the results of all his work with *WOW* and he was ready to tell Charles about them.

Charles was very pleased to see him. In a few moments they were chatting over a coffee, talking about their families and their holiday plans. But soon the chat was over. Charles moved closer towards Jean and asked the question he had been waiting to ask.

'Have you done it, Jean? Have you finished making *WOW*?'

'Yes, I have, Charles,' Jean replied. 'I've completed everything.'

'That's wonderful!' Charles said. 'I've been really excited about this – and, hey, I'm not the only one, oh no! But come on, Jean, tell me everything. Just in a few words. Give me an idea. Well …?'

Jean looked a little uncomfortable, but he lifted up his eyes and looked into Charles's worried face and began, '*WOW* is a liquid which you can't see and you can't smell, a liquid which – in itself – is completely harmless.' Jean could see Charles nodding his head and smiling widely. 'In carefully measured amounts, it can make a person prefer one kind of food or drink over another—'

'Hey, Jean!' Charles cried out. 'That's brilliant! Just what we wanted!'

'I haven't finished, Charles …'

Charles apologised, still nodding his head, and Jean continued.

'However, if these amounts are exceeded … I mean, if we put too much *WOW* into a product,[4] a person can lose control over their appetite for the product. In the worst cases, people will want the product so much that it becomes really dangerous. It could even kill them. The person will eat or drink until they are dead. The person *has* to have the product – they have no choice.'

11

For a moment Charles had stopped smiling. 'So what you're saying is: if we add too much *WOW* to something, it's going to make it dangerous?'

'That's right.'

'But,' Charles continued, 'if the amounts are right, we can use *WOW* safely, right?'

'Well, yes, but—'

'No problem then!' Charles laughed. 'I'm sure it'll be perfectly OK, Jean. I'll make sure everybody understands.'

'No, Charles,' Jean said, more impatiently this time. 'Let me explain. I've been doing some thinking about this lately—'

'You certainly have, Mr Clever!' said Charles. 'And it's about time the company recognised your achievement. I mean, you've made something amazing. We're going to make millions on this one, Jean. Millions!'

'Charles!' Jean raised his voice. 'Let me explain more clearly. *WOW* is dangerous! If it's used in the wrong amounts, it can make people crazy … crazy with a need for … for anything they eat or drink. And then they won't want to eat or drink anything else at all! Look, Charles, even if it *is* used in safe amounts, it gives one product an unfair advantage over another. I mean, shouldn't one apple pie[5] sell better than another because it's a better apple pie and not because we've put some clever additive into it? No, I'm not sure that it should be used at all, even in safe amounts.'

'Now, Jean, just hold on a minute—'

'No, Charles!' Jean shouted. 'Imagine if somebody wanted to use *WOW* as a weapon – as something to hurt people. Imagine if somebody put it into a city's water supply! People would be just like my mice. They would die from drinking too much water!'

'Well,' Charles replied, more calmly now, 'I see your point now, Jean. We have to be careful with these things.'

'At first,' Jean said, 'I was excited by the idea of helping people to eat good food. There are too many fat people these days; I wanted to help with the problems.'

'Oh, yes!' Charles said. 'Of course!'

'Yes, well,' Jean replied as he touched the scar on his cheek, 'I realise now that I was playing with fire. It'll be better if the research⁶ is put away and forgotten about. It's too dangerous and just too … too *wrong*. You can see that now, can't you, Charles?'

'Yes, I can see that, Jean,' Charles said quietly. 'Look, leave this with me. I'll speak to our top people and explain. After all, we can't ask our customers to buy something that's dangerous, can we? No, you did the right thing, Jean; you can't be too careful about these things.'

'I'm pleased you understand, Charles,' said Jean. 'I feel a lot better about things now.'

'Quite right, Jean,' said Charles. 'Listen. Why don't you take the next few weeks off? You and your family could have a good long holiday. You need a rest. And you've earned it.'

'Thank you, Charles – I think I will.'

Jean turned to go.

'Oh, and Jean ...'

'Yes, Charles?'

'Could you just leave all your *WOW* work with me before you go? I'll see that it's all taken care of.'

*　*　*

One year later

Katya was feeling very happy. She and Jean had had two long holidays over the last year – one in Brazil and one in Ireland. Little Alain had really loved them. And Jean was working on some interesting new research into making petrol safer and cleaner. Jean liked doing work that helped people. This new research was his biggest interest at the moment.

Alain was healthier and happier. He was even eating green vegetables! Maybe the fresh air at the Irish beaches had helped. In any case, Katya had discovered some new vegetables in packets which Alain seemed to be very happy with. In fact, he often asked for more.

Katya looked at Alain sleeping happily in the early afternoon. She took out her notebook computer – she was sure she could start work on her book now.

But first she decided she would have some lunch. She had never really liked hamburgers, but she had discovered some recently that were really nice. They were her favourite lunch now. She should watch her weight, really, but … oh, one more burger wouldn't hurt, would it?

Just *one* more.

ACTIVITIES

1 <u>Underline</u> the correct words in each sentence.

1 Jean's additive makes the mice *thirsty* / <u>*want to drink the water*</u>.

2 Katya is worried that her *son's diet isn't healthy* / *son doesn't eat enough*.

3 Jean knows his experiment with *WOW* is finally successful when the mice eat and drink *normally* / *more than usual*.

4 One year later Katya thinks that *Alain's diet is healthier* / *Alain is sleeping better*.

2 Complete the sentences with the names in the box.

> Alain   Charles (x2)   Jean (x2)
> Katya (x2)   The mice

1 _Jean_ has been very careful since a firework exploded in his face when he was a boy.

2 _____ carry on drinking the water with the additive even though it's killing them.

3 _____ tells Jean that he's the company's top chemist.

4 _____ refuses to eat vegetables at the beginning of the story.

5 _____ explains that it would be dangerous if too much *WOW* were used.

6 _____ believes that Jean's additive is going to earn the company a lot of money.

7 _____ thinks that Alain's new liking for vegetables could be a result of the fresh air on holiday.

8 _____ now likes a type of food that she didn't like before.

16

3 What do the <u>underlined</u> words refer to in these lines from the text?

1 He was always careful after <u>that</u>. (page 5)
   the firework exploded in his face

2 'What if,' Jean thought, '<u>these children</u> could be persuaded to eat healthy food?' (page 7)

3 '<u>This</u>,' Jean thought, 'could be a problem.' (page 8)

4 'Hey Jean!' Charles cried out. '<u>That</u>'s brilliant!' (page 11)

5 'No, I'm not sure that <u>it</u> should be used at all, even in safe amounts.' (page 12)

6 In fact, he often asked for <u>more</u>. (page 14)

4 Answer the questions.

1 At first, how does Jean think *WOW* could help people?

2 What does Jean say could happen to people if too much *WOW* is used?

3 Why did Charles ask Jean to leave all his *WOW* work with him?

4 What do you think has happened to change Alain and Katya's taste in food at the end of the story?

Full English Breakfast

Time: *the present*
Place: *Hastings, on the southeast coast of England*

My Aunt Brenda owns a small hotel called the Sea View Guesthouse in Hastings. It's got five bedrooms and it's a very good guesthouse. People come from everywhere to stay there. Hastings is a good place to stay if you want to see the beautiful southeast coast of England. It's an old town. Aunt Brenda's house is over a hundred years old and she has managed it as a guesthouse for the last ten years. Aunt Brenda is a good-looking woman. Everybody says so. She's almost forty years of age with red hair and a mind of her own. Her husband is my Uncle Ralph and he loves her very much. Her guests always like her too.

My Uncle Ralph is a local butcher and he has a shop. The shop is well known in the town. He provides all the meat for the guesthouse. His sausages, Aunt Brenda always says, are the best in England. She always persuades her guests to have them for breakfast. Her 'Full English Breakfast', as she calls it, is famous in Hastings. Brenda's 'Full English Breakfast' includes bacon, eggs, mushrooms, tomatoes, toast and, of course, Uncle Ralph's sausages.

They are the most important part of it. Aunt Brenda takes great pleasure in the fact that all of her guests have tried Ralph's sausages and loved them.

All, that is, except Mr Dunn.

'Don't you worry,' Brenda told me. 'I'll make sure he eats Ralph's sausages before he leaves here. Just you wait and see!'

Aunt Brenda's 'Full English Breakfast' is mentioned in all the holiday web pages. It's the reason why most people stay at the guesthouse. If you don't eat it all, especially the sausages, she thinks you are just being rude. And there is no way she will accept that! She always likes to hear her guests say how much they enjoy the sausages. In fact, she *expects* them to say it.

Now don't think for one moment that Ralph's sausages are anything less than delicious. He makes sausages out of different kinds of meat. They are made in all kinds of different ways and flavours to please all kinds of tastes.

Except Mr Dunn's.

You see, Mr Dunn was a vegetarian. A vegetarian doesn't eat meat at all. No chicken, no beef, no pork and not even any fish. In fact, Mr Dunn didn't even wear leather shoes. Even his sweaters, Brenda tells me, weren't made of wool.

'Now don't tell me that's normal,' Brenda told me. 'We've had vegetarians at the guesthouse before. I always manage to persuade them to have a sausage and once they've had one …' Here Brenda raised her eyes to the ceiling. When she did this, she meant, 'you know what happens next.' And, of course, I do. Nobody has ever tasted Ralph's sausages before and not wanted another. I could see that she wasn't going to let Mr Dunn be the first to refuse. Not if she could help it. I knew then that Mr Dunn, one way or another, was going to eat a sausage.

Me? I'm Claire, Aunt Brenda's niece. I live in Hastings, too, with my mum. My aunt and I have always got on well and I see a lot of her. We both love Hastings. Like many towns by the sea, it has lots of visitors. Some of them are rather strange. Some pass through and some stay. Seaside towns like Hastings seem to interest all kinds of people. I think that's part of the reason we both like Hastings.

But Mr Dunn was stranger than anybody I'd ever seen before.

To begin with, he looked as if he hadn't had a good meal for a long time. He was tall and thin and his hair was as grey as iron. His nose was big and made him look like a wild, hungry eagle. His eyes were deep in his head and his teeth were long and yellow. One thinks of vegetarians as being gentle people. He didn't look gentle at all. He looked like he could kill things with his teeth alone – if he wanted to.

Then there were his hands. They were long and he had thin fingers with thick, sharp fingernails. His fingers looked very strong. I don't know what he did for a living. I wouldn't like to work with him, I'm sure of that!

Mr Dunn was going to be staying at my aunt's house for three weeks. Aunt Brenda had to buy vegetarian stuff just for him, like soya milk. He never had cow's milk. She didn't like that! He always ate his cereal with soya milk for breakfast without speaking to anyone. She didn't like that either.

I have breakfast at Aunt Brenda's place every Saturday morning. She likes to look after her little niece, even though I am already seventeen years old. This Saturday she wanted me to talk to Mr Dunn.

'You see what you can find out about him, Claire!' she told me. 'I want to see him eating a nice sausage, not that soya rubbish! And *please* hurry up. He's already been here for over a week. I've only got ten days left to do it!'

I don't see anything wrong with being a vegetarian, I really don't. But you don't argue with Aunt Brenda.

So, at eight o'clock on Saturday morning, I was sitting across the table from Mr Dunn. I was given my 'Full English Breakfast', complete with Ralph's beautiful sausages, and Mr Dunn had his cereal and soya milk.

'Good morning!' I said cheerfully. 'Lovely day, isn't it?'

Mr Dunn looked up from his bowl. His eyes were big and grey.

'Hmm ...' he replied with a voice that sounded like a bear with a bad throat. The sun was shining. It was early September. It *was* a lovely day.

'Have you tried these sausages?' I asked. 'They really are delicious!'

'I don't eat meat,' he said. 'Not any more.'

'Er … you *used* to eat it then?' I asked.

Mr Dunn gave me a bad-tempered look and then he answered slowly, 'I was told I had to give it up.'

'Er … for health reasons?' I asked.

Mr Dunn almost smiled at me as he raised a corner of his mouth. 'Oh, yes. *My* health … and others' too!'

I heard him make a deep sound that may have been laughter – it was hard to tell with Mr Dunn.

'Surely just *one* sausage wouldn't hurt you?' I said, holding up a piece on my fork, as if to make my point clear. 'They really are good!'

Mr Dunn said nothing, but the look he gave me was enough to make me shut up.

I finished my breakfast and left as soon as I could.

*   *   *

'For *health* reasons?' said Brenda over a cup of tea later that morning. 'Ralph's sausages would be really good for anybody's health! He *needs* a bit of meat if you ask me. It would do him good.'

I could see by the look in her eyes that Brenda was thinking of something. When Brenda starts thinking of something, it usually means trouble for somebody. Usually me.

'You say he *used to* eat meat?' Brenda looked towards me. 'He ate it once; he'll eat it again. I just to have to think of a plan ...'

'Oh, no!' I thought to myself.

*   *   *

Brenda had, of course, tried to interest Mr Dunn in her sausages from the first day he arrived. Every morning she asked him again until he told her not to. That was only on the third day. So Brenda said nothing more and gave him his vegetarian breakfasts. She asked him about himself, just to make conversation. The truth is, Brenda is the kind of person who likes to know other people's business. She didn't get much out of Mr Dunn, but she didn't give up. Eventually, on the Monday of the second week, she got some information out of him.

'So that's what he told me, Claire,' she said. 'He's resting after an illness. He didn't say what it was, but he has to be careful with his diet. I told you he looked ill, didn't I? Anyway, anybody can see that all he needs is some good meat inside him. It would do him a lot of good. You can see in his eyes he wants meat. I've seen him looking at the other guests when they're eating their sausages. You can't tell me he's happy with cereal and soya milk!'

*   *   *

A few days later I stopped at Aunt Brenda's guesthouse to see what was happening with Mr Dunn.

'He's agreed to try a sausage,' my aunt told me excitedly.

'Really?' I said. I was amazed.

'Well, he said he might try a vegetarian sausage,' she said.

'So is Uncle Ralph going to make some?' I asked her.

'Well, that's what I told Mr Dunn,' my aunt replied. 'I said they would be ready on Saturday.' And then she added, 'Oh, and I also said that you would try them first and let him know what they are like!'

But, of course, Brenda was lying about the sausages. Ralph had never made vegetarian sausages in his life and he wasn't going to start now.

'Is this a good idea?' I said to my aunt slowly. 'They're not going to be vegetarian sausages at all: they'll be meat sausages, just like all the others. You're telling *lies* to Mr Dunn, Aunt Brenda!'

'Ah, but he won't know,' said Brenda, looking me in the eye. 'Not if nobody tells him!'

'But why do you care so much?' I asked. 'It's only a sausage!'

I already knew the answer. To Brenda, her 'Full English Breakfast' was what she was known for. It just wasn't a *Full English Breakfast* without Ralph's sausages. And nobody had ever turned down the famous sausages. To turn down Brenda's sausages was to turn *her* down and she didn't like that at all!

I knew then that Mr Dunn didn't have a chance.

* * *

The next Saturday I arrived early at my aunt's guesthouse. I knew what to do. I sat opposite Mr Dunn during breakfast so that he could see the beach through the window. Brenda's guesthouse was also famous for its views of the sea. She thought the sea air helped her guests to enjoy their food more.

There was a street between the guesthouse and the beach and the windows were very big so that people passing by could see everybody enjoying their food. It was good for business.

Mr Dunn looked even more bad-tempered than usual. He seemed to have a cold because he sneezed a lot.

Anyway, soon my aunt came out with my breakfast. It had bacon, egg, mushrooms, tomatoes, toast and Uncle Ralph's 'vegetarian' sausages. All cooked perfectly. Of course, the sausages were meat sausages as usual, but I didn't tell him that.

I started eating my breakfast hungrily.

'They really are *so* delicious,' I said, chewing one of my sausages with a smile.

Mr Dunn looked up. Was he showing some interest at last?

'Amazing,' I said. 'So tasty.'

'And are they completely vegetarian?' he asked.

'Brenda says they are all soya and herbs,[7] but they taste just like the best sausages ever. No meat at all, she says. Nobody could ever tell the difference. Would you like to try one?'

That's when he finally agreed to try one.

Brenda brought in just one meat sausage on a plate. It was beautifully cooked, all golden brown, and it smelled wonderful to me. I'm not sure Mr Dunn could smell it properly with his cold. But he certainly looked at it with hungry eyes.

We watched as Mr Dunn cut a small piece and put it on his fork. He put it to his nose and tried to smell it. He closed his eyes and put it into his mouth. He chewed it for a few seconds and smiled.

Brenda smiled at me. It had worked! Mr Dunn liked them!

Suddenly, Mr Dunn made a horrible sound, like an animal. He stood up and held his throat tightly. We watched as he seemed to grow in front of us. One moment he was Mr Dunn, the next moment he was bigger, greyer and … hairier. His ears grew and his face got longer. He cried out, just like a wolf, and jumped up from his chair.

Then he jumped across the table and straight through the window. There was a huge crash as broken glass was sent flying all over the street. He landed outside and looked around like a frightened animal. He went down onto his hands – if they were still hands – and ran straight into the road and the busy morning traffic. We couldn't see him. We heard a crash and I heard some people scream. A bus stopped suddenly.

When we went outside, we expected to see Mr Dunn lying in front of the bus. We saw the driver standing in the road.

'Where did that thing come from?' he asked. 'I mean, just look at the size of it!'

'*He* is a *man* staying at my aunt's guesthouse,' I told the driver without looking. 'He came out of there. His name is—'

'Man? What are you talking about?' said the driver. 'Just take a look at it!'

Aunt Brenda and I looked. There, lying dead on the ground, was the body of a huge grey dog. Its mouth was open and it had long yellow teeth. Its feet, or rather paws, were huge with thick sharp claws. It was bigger than any dog I'd ever seen in my life.

'That's a wolf!' somebody shouted.

They were right: it *was* a wolf. But what was a wolf doing on a busy road in Hastings?

*   *   *

We never saw Mr Dunn again. Nobody knew anything about him. We never found out who he really was.

Or, indeed, *what* he really was.

Aunt Brenda still manages her guesthouse and cooks her 'Full English Breakfast', but she doesn't mind if her guests want cereal instead of sausages now.

In fact, I think she prefers it.

ACTIVITIES

1 Complete the summary of the story with the names in the box.

> Brenda (x3) Ralph Mr Dunn (x4) Claire (x2)

Claire's Aunt ¹ _Brenda_ owns a small guesthouse next to the beach in Hastings. The guesthouse is famous for its 'Full English Breakfast', especially its sausages, which Brenda's husband, ² .... , makes. When ³ .... , a vegetarian, comes to stay for three weeks, ⁴ .... gets very annoyed because he refuses to eat her famous sausages. She offers him one every morning, but he always refuses. Brenda's niece, ⁵ .... , tries to persuade him too, but without success. Finally, ⁶ .... tells Mr Dunn that Ralph will make him a special vegetarian sausage without any meat. However, this isn't true: what she gives him is actually a normal meat sausage. After eating only one piece of it, there is a terrible change in ⁷ .... and he suddenly jumps out of the window and into the street. There is a big crash outside as somebody is hit by a bus. ⁸ .... and her aunt go out, expecting to see ⁹ .... lying in front of the bus, but when they get there, they see it is actually a wolf that has been killed. What happened to ¹⁰ .... ?

2 What do the <u>underlined</u> words refer to in these lines from the text?

1 'I always manage to persuade <u>them</u> to have a sausage and once they've had one ...' (page 20) _vegetarians_

2 'I was told I had to give <u>it</u> up.' (page 23) ....

3 '<u>It</u> would do him good.' (page 24) ....

4 'Well <u>that</u>'s what I told Mr Dunn,' my aunt replied. (page 25)

....

5 He closed his eyes and put <u>it</u> into his mouth. (page 26)

....

6 <u>Its</u> mouth was open and it had long yellow teeth. (page 29)

....

3 Complete the information from a holiday web site.

http://www.seaviewguesthousehotel.com

Sea View Guesthouse
Where? ¹ ...., southeast England
What? Small seaside hotel with five ² .... You'll get a warm welcome from the owner of this small hotel, Brenda Brown. But don't turn down her famous ³ ....! Start your day with a plate of ⁴ ...., eggs, mushrooms, ⁵ ...., toast – and, most important of all, the speciality ⁶ ...., made by her husband Ralph, a local ⁷ .... A great place to stay, but better for meat-eaters than ⁸ ....!

4 Answer the questions.

1 Why did Mr Dunn smile when he tried the sausage?

....

2 How does Brenda change at the end of the story?

....

31

A Little Pot of Honey

In the late nineteenth century, there were many foreigners in China. In some areas of the country, they seemed to rule almost every part of Chinese society. Some Chinese people were very unhappy about this and started a special group or society to fight the foreigners. The people in this society were called Boxers because some of them studied Chinese martial arts. Martial arts were their special ways of fighting. They fought against the foreigners from 1899 to 1901. This time in history is known as the Boxer Rebellion.

Time: *1901*
Place: *A temple[8] in Shandong province, China*

The old man walked into his room. The door was already open. Immediately, he saw the small broken pots on the floor and tears of sadness and anger filled his eyes. He was too late.

The pots were not worth anything, of course. But they had contained the last of his honey. His special honey, made by his own bees. It was the honey that had given his students – the Boxers – their strength. If a student ate some of this special honey, he became really strong for a short time. But no amount of strength could stop the guns. His students were now all dead. Now the foreigners took what they wanted.

But the old man would not let them take everything. He had saved one very small pot of honey in his pocket. One day he would give it as a present to the Emperor[9] of China. Now he had to hide it.

The old man heard heavy footsteps outside. It was the foreign soldiers. He put his little pot into a wooden box of small presents that he had saved for the Emperor. He hid the box in the corner of his room and then turned towards the door. He walked into the bright morning sunshine for the last time.

*   *   *

Time: *the present*
Place: *Sweetbourne, a small town in Kansas, USA*

Jack Rawlins put his hand up to his black eye as he walked into the kitchen of his home. He knew his eye looked bad.

'Another black eye, son?' asked Evan Rawlins, Jack's dad.

He expected Jack to get a few injuries in a school football match, but it had happened too many times lately. He knew why: it was Rex Coulter, the college bully. He was the only one who would want to give Jack a black eye.

'I guess so, Dad. But I did get the winning points!'

Evan Rawlins smiled at his son. Jack was sixteen, almost a man, and he was popular at school. He was a good footballer too, but Evan knew that Jack and all of his friends were being bullied during football matches. Everyone knew that the college bully was Rex Coulter. There was nothing Evan could do. There was nothing the other parents could do either. Boys play rough games. Boy? Rex Coulter was eighteen and he was big. He had short blond hair and a big nose and he must have weighed at least one hundred and ten kilos. He wasn't as good at football as Jack was, but he was strong and fast. And he liked to hurt people.

Evan put his arm round his son.

'How about doing something to take your mind away from football?'

Jack smiled. His dad bought and sold houses and he often bought everything inside them too. Jack liked the houses, especially when they were old. He loved looking through the things that were in old houses because sometimes, just sometimes, there was something really interesting there.

'You want me to look through some old stuff again, right?' asked Jack.

'Only if you want to, son.'

'When do I start?'

'First thing tomorrow morning. But first, let's look at that eye!'

* * *

35

The house that Jack's father had bought was at the other side of town. An English army officer had built the house in 1930 and his family had lived there ever since. The army officer's granddaughter, now an old lady, had been the last person from that same family to live there.

Jack parked next to a large tree in front of the house. He looked up at the building. For a town like Sweetbourne, it was an old house. And it looked old too. Inside, the rooms were in poor condition. This wasn't unusual in big old houses. But there was one room that was especially unusual. It was the biggest room on the ground floor. It was dark and full of old furniture. It was like a museum. There were old photographs on the wall of soldiers and places in other countries. One photograph showed a smiling army officer standing next to some Chinese men. The Chinese men's hands were tied and they looked unhappy. Were they prisoners? The officer was wearing a British uniform. Was he the man who had built this house? Jack thought so.

The shelves were full of things from China and India – old coins and photographs, old pots and pieces of art and even some dangerous-looking knives. Jack loved these old things and enjoyed looking at them. He could tell that this room contained many unusual and, perhaps, valuable things. Then there, in the corner of one shelf, was a simple little pot that didn't look unusual or valuable at all. Jack looked closer. It was very small, about the size of an egg. It was brown with a small red and black bee painted on its side. Jack picked it up and saw that it had a top which was tightly shut. Nobody had tried to open it – maybe nobody thought it was worth opening. 'Well,' thought Jack, 'my dad owns this now and he told me to look at things, so I'll open it!'

At first the pot was difficult to open, but after Jack tried a little harder, the top came off. Jack looked inside the pot and saw, much to his surprise, that there was a small amount of thick, golden liquid inside. It smelled sweet. He knew at once what the smell was – it was honey! Even though there wasn't much there, Jack couldn't help putting his finger in and tasting it. It tasted delicious, with an unusual, flowery taste that he couldn't recognise. He wanted to finish it all, but he had work to do. He would save it for later.

Jack put the pot down on a shelf and decided to take a walk round the house to see what the garden was like. There was an old tree stump in the garden which he had to pass. There wasn't much space and he hit his leg against the stump. He cried out, more in anger than in pain, and kicked against the stump. He was surprised to see that the stump flew into the air and landed at the other end of the garden.

He went over to look at it. The old dead stump, Jack thought, must have gone soft in the ground. He looked at

the stump. It wasn't soft at all. The roots were dead, but they were still there and the stump looked hard and heavy. He looked again and he saw that the roots had been torn out of the ground. Had *he* done that? Looking again at the size and weight of the stump, Jack guessed that he couldn't even lift it. He tried and found to his great surprise that he could lift it – easily. It was as light as a pillow! He dropped the stump onto the ground and the sound it made, as well as the hole it made in the ground, showed that the stump was very heavy indeed.

'Whoo-hoo!' Jack shouted.

He didn't know how, but he had suddenly become as strong as twenty men, maybe more! Jack went to his dad's car, which was large and new and had a big engine. He put his hands under the front of the car and lifted. It came up as easily as lifting a chair. For the next ten minutes Jack went around the house lifting every heavy thing he found. He was enjoying himself. Then, suddenly, when he tried to lift up a large stone in the garden, he couldn't move it a single centimetre. He tried his best, but it was no good: Jack's amazing new strength had left him as quickly as he'd found it.

He was normal again.

'It was that honey!' Jack said to himself. 'It had to be.'

For some reason, the honey had given him great strength for a few minutes. Jack ran back to find the pot. There it was, still on the shelf. He closed the pot and put it into his pocket. He decided that it would be his secret until he decided what he would do with it. He wouldn't give it to his dad, at least, not yet. Maybe that *would* be the right thing to do. 'But not just yet,' Jack thought. 'First I'll have some fun with it!'

* * *

Jack finished looking at the house and found plenty of other interesting things. But all day he thought about the honey in his pocket. When he got home, he told his father about the house. Dad was pleased when he heard about all the old and unusual things Jack had found in the house. But Jack didn't tell him about the honey.

'You've worked hard today, son,' he told Jack. And he gave Jack a fifty-dollar note. 'Go out and have some fun,' he added.

Jack was feeling good. He had money and he had friends to enjoy it with.

And he had his little pot of honey.

* * *

The morning was fine and sunny. It was early summer and Jack was enjoying a walk through the streets of Sweetbourne with a few of his friends from the football team. They were going to go to the local swimming pool at the sports centre.

They were just going into the sports centre, when they saw a large young man walking towards them. It was Rex Coulter. On his way he pushed into Jack and almost knocked him down.

'Hey, Rawlins! Watch where you're going!' Rex called out.

'You meant to do that!' Jack told him.

'I didn't see a little guy like you' said Rex. 'You need to go to the gym and exercise a bit more if you want me to see you. You're so small I didn't notice you.'

Jack was quite tall and he was healthy and strong too. But next to Rex he did look small. Most people did, especially sixteen-year-old kids.

But Jack was tired of Rex Coulter.

'Why don't you just shut up, Rex?' Jack told him.

Jack's friends went quiet. Had he gone crazy? They looked worried.

Rex laughed. 'Oh, yeah? Do you want to fight me and see? How about it, tough guy? Right now, huh?'

Jack was feeling angry, but he wasn't feeling stupid.

A street fight would just get Jack into trouble. He didn't want that. He wanted to fight Rex, but in some sport with rules. He wanted to make Rex look bad in front of everybody. But what sport could he choose? Jack had an idea.

'Look,' Jack said. 'Everyone knows you're good at wrestling – you're the best at college, right? Well, how about a wrestling match – you against me?'

Rex could hardly believe what he was hearing. 'Are you serious? I'm good – very good. After five minutes with me in a wrestling match, you'll know what "good" means.'

'Oh, I'm serious, believe me,' Jack said.

Jack's friends were trying to stop him, telling him he was crazy. But Jack just put up his hands and called out loudly, 'Look, I'm tired of Rex bullying people. I'll win this wrestling match, just you wait and see.'

Jack turned to Rex. 'So, we do this right and stick to the wrestling rules, OK?'

Rex was amazed. 'OK, my trainer will be the referee.[10] I won't be allowed to kick your teeth in or hit you in your other eye. I'll be happy just to tie your legs around your head and throw you around a little. You can just worry about avoiding me, OK Shorty?' Rex was laughing now. He was enjoying himself. 'If you can avoid me for three minutes,' he continued, 'I'll shake your hand and apologise. But that's not going to happen. Anyway, how about three o'clock? At the sports centre?'

Jack's friends were all trying to persuade Jack to leave and telling him not to be crazy. But Jack didn't want to stop.

'Three o'clock. I'll be there,' he replied.

Rex left, laughing loudly.

Jack was popular around school and Rex wasn't. Jack's friends thought he was quite mad, but they liked him and didn't want to see him get hurt by Rex Coulter.

Soon the news was everywhere. Jack's friends had made up their minds that they were going to help him.

'Look,' said Eddie Kowalski, Jack's best friend. 'If you get into serious trouble, me and all the guys will jump into the wrestling ring and help – don't worry.'

'Thanks, Eddie,' said Jack. 'That means a lot to me. Now, how about a swim?'

* * *

Dad was away looking at a house in the next town. Jack was pleased that Dad didn't know about the wrestling match yet.

He wouldn't hear about it until it was all over. Then, later, he would be very happy to hear that his son had won a wrestling match against Rex Coulter! With the help of that little pot of honey, Jack just couldn't lose. Even if he didn't know about wrestling, he could just pick up Rex and throw him out of the room if he wanted to. And he *did* want to.

Everybody wanted Rex Coulter to lose a match. It would be good for him to find out what losing was like for a change.

Jack was actually looking forward to it.

At two o'clock Jack got his things and walked towards the sports centre. It was still a fine day. The pot of honey was ready in his pocket. Eddie met him as he got to the high street.

'I've told everybody to come. They'll all be there, Jack.'

'Hey, thanks, Eddie. Thanks very much.'

'You know, Jack, we all think you're crazy to do this, but we love you for it. You know that, right?'

'I know. Thanks.'

'And I meant what I said before – we'll come and help you if you really get in trouble.'

'That's good to know, Eddie. Thanks,' said Jack.

'Hey,' Eddie asked, 'do you want to come in my car? I'm just going to pick up some of the other guys and you can come too if you like.'

'I think I'll walk. I'd like to clear my head a little,' Jack answered. 'I'll see you there, OK?'

'Right, Jack,' said Eddie.

'If you'd had a clear head earlier, you wouldn't be in this mess!' That was what Eddie thought to himself, but he didn't tell his friend. It was too late for that. 'See you later. Good luck!' Eddie said.

Jack was alone. He wanted to be by himself for a while. He was sure the honey would work, but he still felt nervous. After all, Rex was fast and strong – and big! And Jack didn't know a thing about wrestling. He felt in his pocket for the fifteenth time. Yes, it was still there. With the help of the honey, he couldn't lose against Rex.

Suddenly, there was a loud, dull bang and it sounded like it came from nearby. What was it? Jack heard people screaming. He looked up the street and soon saw what it was: a woman was inside a car. The car had hit a wall and smoke was coming from the engine. It looked like the woman couldn't get out. Somebody shouted that a little boy had run into the road and the car had crashed to avoid him. The smell of petrol was everywhere. The woman was screaming. A man was trying to open her door. The car was burning and there was no way out. It was a horrible situation. Where were the firefighters? Nobody knew.

Jack knew what he had to do. He got out his honey pot and opened it. There was only a small amount of honey. He needed some to fight Rex. But he also needed to save this woman. He decided at once that her life was more important and ate all of it. He couldn't take any chances if he was to be sure of saving the woman.

Jack ran over to the car and pushed his way through the crowd of people. He could see fire moving now, from the front of the car towards the woman inside. He had to move quickly. He got to the door, held onto the handle and pulled. The whole door came off and the woman fell out. Jack helped her to run away from the burning car.

Ten seconds later the car exploded.

'You saved my life!' the woman cried. 'But how did you …? The door … I mean … it wouldn't move!'

'I guess I just got the lock in the right position.' Jack looked at her: with her blonde hair and large nose, now dirty with smoke, she reminded him of somebody.

'What's your name, son?' she asked.

Jack told her. Then he hurried off before she could say anything else.

'I'm late for something – I've got to go! Bye!' he shouted.

Jack ran down the street. It was almost three o'clock and he had a wrestling match. But what was he going to do? – he had used up all of his honey! He couldn't fight Rex without it! But wait – maybe, just maybe it was still working. Jack looked around for something to test himself on. He saw a parked car and tried to lift the front of it. It was no good – he just couldn't move it.

Jack was back to his normal strength and he had no more of the honey left.

Rex Coulter was going to break his bones like biscuits in front of everybody. And there was nothing he could do about it.

He could just go home, of course. But Jack didn't consider that for one moment. No, he would have to wrestle Rex Coulter, if only to show his friends that one should never give in to bullies. Not even huge and very strong bullies. He started to walk more slowly.

The sports centre was near now, and many of his friends were already there. In fact, there was already quite a crowd.

'There he is!' somebody cried.

Everyone shouted happily.

'Wow,' thought Jack. 'I really do have a lot of fans. We haven't even started wrestling yet! They should at least wait until I've tried to fight Rex.'

Jack remembered that Eddie had told him his friends might save him from real trouble. Maybe he would be OK after all.

Then Jack noticed Rex Coulter. He seemed to be shouting more loudly than anyone else. He was pushing through the crowd towards Jack, holding a mobile phone and speaking to someone.

Rex came up to Jack and hugged him hard. Rex was repeating the words 'thank you, thank you,' again and again.

'Is Rex almost crying?' thought Jack.

Then Jack realised who the woman had reminded him of. And he realised who he had saved from the burning car.

Rex Coulter's mother.

ACTIVITIES

1 Complete the sentences with the names in the box.

> Jack (x3)   Rex (x3)   The Boxers
> Evan (x2)   Eddie

1 _The Boxers_ were all killed a long time ago.
2 _____ was hurt in a football match.
3 _____ is the college bully.
4 _____ buys and sells houses.
5 _____ finds some magic honey.
6 _____ gives away some money.
7 _____ offers to help his friend.
8 _____ saves a woman's life.
9 _____ gets a call on his mobile phone.
10 _____ hugs someone he was going to fight.

2 Are the sentences true (*T*) or false (*F*)?

1 The old man gives a present to the Emperor of China. ☐F
2 Evan doesn't know that his son is getting bullied. ☐
3 Jack finds lots of old things from China and India in the house that his father bought. ☐
4 Jack finds his dad's car easy to lift. ☐
5 Jack wants to fight Rex in a sport with rules. ☐
6 Evan knows about the fight his son is planning. ☐
7 The woman in the car hits a child that has run into the road. ☐
8 Jack uses up all the honey before he gets to the sports centre. ☐

3 **Match the two parts of the sentences.**

1 The honey was [e]
2 Jack's father often [ ]
3 An English army officer and his family [ ]
4 The Chinese people in the old photo [ ]
5 Rex is so big that he [ ]
6 Jack's friends tell him [ ]
7 The woman can't [ ]
8 At the end of the story, Rex [ ]

a escape from the car by herself.
b changes his behaviour towards Jack.
c used to live in the house that Evan bought.
d buys a house with all the things inside.
e made a long time ago in China.
f were probably prisoners.
g makes other kids look small.
h not to fight Rex.

4 **Answer the questions.**

1 Who built the old house that Jack's father has bought?

....

2 How does Jack discover that the honey could make him strong?

....

3 What do Jack's friends do when he tells Rex to shut up?

....

4 Why does Jack want to fight Rex, even without the magic honey?

....

5 Who is the woman that Jack saves from the car?

....

Kung Fu Spice

I kicked a stone into the road as I walked home. My confidence was low and I was feeling pretty sorry for myself. I felt like a failure at seventeen years of age.

I was no good at anything. OK, I could cook, but nobody at school thought cooking was cool. Not unless you were on

TV. That wasn't going to happen. Not to me.

'Ah, well,' I told myself, 'so Alex Chen is never going to be one of life's stars.'

I was nearly home. I was thinking about food. My home is The Golden Dragon, one of the best Chinese restaurants in Liverpool, so I think of food a lot. I cooked here at weekends for my dad. Dad always said I was a really good cook. He even said I was good enough to enter the *Young Cook of the Year* competition on TV. But I wasn't sure. I mean, I liked cooking, but did I want to *be* a cook? Well, yes I did – but I wanted to be the best. I wasn't sure I could be that.

So far, I'd never been the best at anything. The school football team had turned me down. I had failed my driving test. Huh! If only I could be the best at *something*.

* * *

'The trouble with young people today,' said Grandmother as she helped herself yet again to the chicken and rice I had cooked, 'is that they don't care about the old ways and traditions.[11] Nobody cares about old people any more.'

By 'young people' she meant me and my dad and by 'old people' she meant herself. Grandmother was the oldest person in the Chen family and she came from Hong Kong every February to see Dad, Mum and me for Chinese New Year.

'A son should visit his mother – not the other way round. Isn't that the way in England, too, Delia, dear?'

'I'm from Liverpool,' said Mum. 'Don't ask me about the rest of England. I've been married to George for eighteen years now and I still don't understand how they do things in Hong Kong.'

Dad smiled. It was the same every year. Grandmother and Mum always pretended to act as if they didn't understand each other, when we all knew they did really.

'And you know how busy the restaurant is at this time,' said Dad. 'Nearly every Chinese family in Liverpool eats out at Chinese New Year. That's when we make most money. And it pays for you to come here, doesn't it, Mother?'

'Maybe so,' said Grandmother. 'But young Alex always stays here for Christmas with the English side of his family—'

'That would be me,' said Mum.

'But he never has Chinese New Year in Hong Kong. He's fifteen now—'

'Seventeen,' I reminded her. I always have to remind her how old I am.

'As I said,' Grandmother continued, 'he needs to get in touch with his own traditions.'

'Yeah, I know,' I said. 'But I can do both, can't I? I mean, I was born here, not in Hong Kong. But I still see Hong Kong nearly every summer. And Dad, you make sure I know everything about the place.'

'Everything?' said Grandmother. 'You still can't speak Chinese very well.'

'Neither can Dad,' I said.

'I've just got out of practice, that's all,' Dad answered.

'All right, everybody,' said Mum. 'Relax. Grandmother, we make sure Alex knows about both sides of his family.'

'Really?' Grandmother asked. 'How much does he know about my little brother, his Great Uncle Tong Po?'

'Mother,' Dad said quietly. 'Even I don't know much about Uncle Tong Po. I've only seen him in a few old photographs. Why do you mention him now?'

'Because,' said Grandmother with a big smile, 'he's coming to see us. He'll be here tomorrow morning!'

I'd never heard of Great Uncle Tong Po. Neither had Mum.

'Excuse me,' Mum said. 'Why hasn't anybody ever told me about Great Uncle Tong Po?'

Grandmother was loving every minute of this little drama. She chewed a piece of chicken thoughtfully and then she began.

'My little brother, Tong Po, ran away from home when he was fourteen,' she said. 'He wanted to join one of the temples in China to be a priest[12] and study martial arts, you know, kung fu. I didn't believe him. But he did run away and we never saw or heard from him for years. Mother and Father pretended to forget him, but I don't think they ever did. In those days people didn't ask many questions about young men who ran away from home. It happened all the time. None of us heard from him. Mother and Father both died just a few years later.'

I thought this was fantastic! A relative who was a Chinese priest who studied martial arts? Cool!

'So, Grandmother,' I asked, 'was he a priest?'

'Well, he sent me a letter about ten years ago. He said he would see me one day. The letter was from the Shaolin Temple in China – that's where they study Chinese martial arts. So I suppose that's what he did. I wrote to him, telling him all about my family – including you, Alex. He never wrote back. Then this morning I got another letter from him. He said he was coming to see us!'

'A letter from the Shaolin Temple?' I said. 'Wow!'

'No, Alex,' Grandmother said, 'it was from London. He's in London and he's going to come to Liverpool by train. He's going to get a taxi here when he gets to Liverpool station. He'll be here by ten o'clock tomorrow morning. He wants to stay for a month – maybe more. There was no time to write back but I knew you wouldn't mind, of course.'

'Of course,' said Mum, with a small smile.

'Does he speak English, Mother?' Dad asked.

'He spoke English as a boy,' said Grandmother, 'though we mostly spoke in Chinese. You can practise your Chinese, can't you?'

'Don't expect me to!' said Mum.

'Don't worry,' Grandmother laughed. 'We'll tell you what he's saying, right?'

Dad and I looked at each other. We were going to spend a month or more with a Shaolin priest in the centre of Liverpool during Chinese New Year.

I could hardly wait to tell my friends at school!

* * *

On Saturday mornings I usually get up early and help out in the restaurant. I cook for the lunchtime customers.

We get a lot of Chinese customers at this time of year. It was no surprise when a Chinese man of about sixty sat down for breakfast. He was small and fat with very short black hair and he looked smart in a dark suit. I watched with interest as he ate the dumplings I had made. I was really good at making dumplings.

He saw me looking.

'Did you make these?' he asked in English with a Chinese accent.

'Yes, sir,' I answered. 'I hope they're OK?'

'Too much salt,' he said quietly. 'They are good but use less salt.'

'Sorry, sir,' I said, thinking he didn't know what he was talking about.

'Here,' he said, picking a dumpling up with his Chinese chopsticks. 'You try – and then tell me if I'm wrong. What tastes stronger, the dumpling or the salt?'

I took the dumpling and put it into my mouth. I thought about it as I chewed. He was right – I'd made them quickly. I never questioned how good they were. They *were* just a little too salty.

'You see?' he said. 'Only a good cook would know the difference. And I can tell you're a good cook, Alex Chen.'

I heard gentle laughter behind me. It was Mum and Dad and Grandmother.

'Listen to your Great Uncle Tong Po, Alex!' said Dad. 'He especially wanted to taste your dumplings!'

Uncle Tong Po! I was expecting somebody who looked like Bruce Lee, but he looked like … well … like Grandmother but fatter.

Dad closed the restaurant while we all joined Uncle Tong Po round the table. I felt shy in front of him. Even though I've never done martial arts myself, I've always liked watching the kung fu films. And this man knew all about Shaolin kung fu and he was sitting right next to me! I didn't know what to say.

'I used to make these dumplings all the time at the Shaolin Temple,' Uncle Tong Po said. 'I see you know something about cooking too, Alex.'

'Thank you, Uncle,' I said. 'But you must know all about different kinds of kung fu from the temple,' I asked. 'What were you best at?'

'I was best at kung fu cooking!' he laughed. 'I could cook a complete meal in under three minutes!'

He was joking, right?

'You were at the Shaolin Temple for many years, weren't you, Uncle?' Dad asked. 'I think Alex is interested in your kung fu fighting. After all, the Shaolin Temple is famous for teaching kung fu – you know, teaching you to fight with your hands and feet.'

Uncle smiled. 'Yes, but all kung fu means is "a thing done well". And what I did well was cook!'

'Cooking?' I asked. 'But you're a Shaolin kung fu teacher, aren't you?'

'Yes,' said Uncle. 'I teach kung fu cooking!'

Maybe I wouldn't tell my school friends about my great uncle the Shaolin kung fu teacher after all – not if he was only a cook!

'Little brother Tong Po,' said Grandmother. 'It's so good to see you. But now you're here, what are your plans?'

'I'm going to spend time with my family and I'm going to teach Alex some Chinese cooking!'

'Alex is already pretty good, you know, Uncle,' said Dad.

Uncle stood up and said, 'Show me the kitchen and give me a few minutes.'

I showed him the kitchen. Then we waited.

After just a few minutes, Uncle came out with a bowl of dumplings.

'Eat!' he told us. So we each took a dumpling and put it into our mouths.

I was used to good dumplings, but these were absolutely delicious. They were the best dumplings I had ever tasted in the whole of my life. I could tell by everyone's faces that they all felt the same.

'So what do you think of your own dumplings now, Alex?' Uncle asked.

Compared to these beautiful dumplings, mine were awful. They had none of the magical taste of Uncle's wonderful dumplings.

'I don't know how you did it, Uncle,' I said. 'I could never cook something that good; never in a million years.'

'All good cooks say that when they first taste real cooking,' Uncle said. 'I know I did.'

I looked down. I didn't know what to say.

'We start tomorrow!' Uncle said. 'But first, I'd like to have some rice wine with my big sister!'

*   *   *

Sundays used to be relaxing. Not any more. Now I got up early and Uncle taught me his cooking.

The first day Uncle made me cook something by myself while he watched. I cooked one of my favourite meat recipes. When I had finished, I put the food in front of him. Then I watched as he tasted it. I looked on nervously. It was the best I could do. I hoped he liked it.

'Too much spice,' he said. 'Spices are added to give more flavour – not take it away. And the meat isn't cooked enough.'

'OK,' I thought to myself, 'you do better!'

Uncle just said, 'Wait here for a few minutes!'

I did. A few minutes later he brought me exactly the same thing. I say *exactly*, but, of course, it wasn't. Uncle's meat with spice was the best I'd *ever* tasted. The meat was soft and there was just the right amount of spice. It was a meal made with a true love of cooking.

I thought I could never cook like that. I felt like giving up.

Uncle put his arm round me.

'Now,' he said, 'the lessons begin.'

*   *   *

The first week was awful. I tried to do things in the same way as Uncle. I wanted to look good, but I was nervous. I got things wrong. My food tasted just the same as it always did.

'Start trying to love the food,' he said. 'Enjoy yourself. Feel happy about your cooking!'

But I didn't feel happy. I felt terrible.

'It's no good, Uncle!' I told him. 'I'll never be able to cook like you. I don't know how you do it. It's like magic. I just don't know your secret.'

Uncle nodded and smiled.

'Ah,' he said. 'You've finally worked it out. I knew you would. You're a smart boy.'

Worked it out? Smart boy? I didn't know what he was talking about. Was I smart? I said nothing.

'You don't think I was a Shaolin priest for nothing, do you? I mean – we have secrets, we know things, we know all about spices – secret spices. Magical spices.'

Magical spices? I didn't know if Uncle was being serious or not. But then, he *was* Shaolin …

'Once I have prepared my food in the right way, it's ready for my secret kung fu spice!' he said with a smile. 'Come, you watch me as I prepare some spicy chicken with rice. You must do everything exactly as I do. Everything. If you do it right, I will add some of my kung fu spice and then your food will be as good as mine.'

Great! Uncle had some special Shaolin spice that made his cooking so good. I wanted it too!

I watched everything he did. I measured everything in exactly the same way, I cooked for the same amount of time, at the same temperature – I did everything the same. In fact, I really enjoyed cooking the meal.

I felt certain that my food was perfectly cooked this time.

Then I saw Uncle do something very strange: he took a small leather bag from his pocket, put in his thumb and finger and took out a little bit of some powder. He sprinkled it over his finished food, and then sprinkled some over mine. I only saw a tiny amount fall from his fingers. I couldn't see it when it was on the food.

'Taste mine first!' Uncle told me.

I tasted a mouthful. It was so delicious that I could hardly imagine anybody else producing anything as good.

'Now taste your own,' Uncle said.

Mine looked the same, but I didn't believe that it could taste the same. When I put the food into my mouth, my eyes opened wide with wonder. It tasted just as good as Uncle's food! I was so happy that Uncle laughed.

'You see!' said Uncle. 'If you prepare the food with love, that's when you can add a little bit of kung fu spice. Nothing will taste finer then! But it's our secret, yes? You mustn't tell anybody about the secrets of the Shaolin Temple, right?'

'Yes, Uncle. I won't tell anybody.'

'Now, come – we have much to study if you are to learn the secret ways of a Shaolin cook!'

* * *

The next few weeks were the busiest I had ever had in my life. I was doing my school work. I was cooking for Dad in the restaurant. And I was learning everything I could from Uncle.

I thought I already knew a lot. But soon I realised I knew very little. I learned how to measure food. I learned what to add to it to give it extra flavour – including spices. I learned about every meat, fish and vegetable. I learned how to make simple food tasty.

Every time I cooked some food, Uncle added a little bit of kung fu spice from his bag.

After a while, Uncle said I was doing very well indeed. But I still wanted to know about Uncle and his time at the Shaolin Temple. I asked him again if he had ever learned about real kung fu.

'I told you before,' he said. 'Kung fu just means "something done well" – it doesn't matter what is studied. But, Alex, I have a present for you.'

'A present?' I asked.

Uncle put a small leather bag on the kitchen table. It was just like the one he used.

'Take it!' he said. 'It's kung fu spice – it's yours. Be careful how you use it – not too much – just a tiny bit with every meal. If you cook with love, the spice will work. It won't if you don't!'

'Wow! Thanks, Uncle! Can I look at it?'

'If you want to, but take care – it's too valuable to waste!'

I opened the bag and looked inside. It was a small bag and inside was some white powder. It certainly didn't look special. It didn't smell of anything much either. But that didn't matter to me. I knew it was the secret Shaolin magic of a real Shaolin priest!

'This will last you a long time if you use it carefully,' he told me. 'But you must cook the way I taught you. You must cook with love – or it won't work.'

'Will it work on any food or is it just Chinese food?' I asked. I wondered about this because my mum made brilliant English and French food. I enjoyed cooking that too.

'If you cook any food with love, it will work,' Uncle said. 'Your kung fu spice will make it the best it can be!'

I put my bag of spice away in my room. I had never forgotten about Dad's idea about the *Young Cook of the Year* competition on TV. I asked Dad about it and he thought it was a great idea. We emailed my entry form the next day. I was feeling confident now. After all, with my kung fu spice, how could I lose?

*　*　*

'Alex! It's a letter!' Mum called.

It was morning and I was still in bed.

'It looks like it's from the TV people!'

I ran downstairs, took the letter from the table and tore it open.

Everybody was watching me.

'Well …?' asked Dad.

'Yes!' I shouted. 'They've said I'm going to be in the *Young Cook of the Year* competition! The first part is next week!'

Mum hugged me, Dad shook my hand, Grandmother kissed me on the nose and Uncle smiled.

'Hey,' I said. 'It's not going to be easy. If I'm going to win this, I have to beat[13] the best young cooks in the country!'

I looked at Uncle and knew that, with the help of his kung fu spice, nobody could beat me.

*   *   *

Time flew by. I worked hard. The first part of the competition was held in Liverpool for the northwest of England – my part of the country. All the other young cooks were having their competitions around the rest of England. I won my part easily with my Chinese cooking. It was fun! But I made sure that with every meal I added a tiny bit of kung fu spice. I didn't tell anybody about that, of course. It just looked like I was putting on a last bit of salt or something. But it worked. They all loved my cooking – and so did I.

The next part of the competition was in London. If I got through that, I would be in the final on TV.

Mum, Dad, Grandmother and Uncle had come to the first part of the competition. I wanted them to be there for me in London too. With my kung fu spice I couldn't fail.

The best young cooks in the country were all in the competition. I had to beat them all. I felt nervous. It was a big day! My family had to wait at our hotel, which was nearby. If I got through this part of the competition, they would see me on TV in the finals.

I was with five other young cooks from all around the country. We all had to cook in a top London restaurant and we were going to be judged[14] by one of the top cooks in London. I wasn't going to cook Chinese food. I didn't mind. I could cook most things now. With my kung fu spice I could cook anything!

We were taken to the kitchen of the restaurant. The head

cook gave us our instructions. He told us that we each had to cook one course of a meal. I had to cook steak with potatoes and green beans. Steak wasn't food I cooked often, but I knew how it was done. We had less than one hour to get the meal ready.

No problem.

I knew exactly what to do for a course like this. I knew how steak should be cooked – not too much, not too little. I knew how to cook potatoes and vegetables so that they were just right. I did everything right. But the main thing was this: I felt good cooking the food. I enjoyed myself.

Soon, the food was ready.

All I needed next was my kung fu spice to make everything perfect. Just a tiny bit was all I needed. I reached for the little bag in my pocket.

It wasn't there!

I searched all of my pockets, but I just couldn't find it. What could I do? I felt afraid. The skin on my back went cold and my tongue went dry. I wanted to run out and find my uncle. He *must* have some more kung fu spice – I had to have it. I had to!

But it was too late. The judge was already on his way to taste my food. Oh, no! Without my Shaolin magic I was just an ordinary cook. What chance did I have of winning now?

The competition judge was French. He looked like he knew everything about cooking. He looked at my steak and cut off a piece. He put some potato on the same fork and some green beans as well. Then he put it all into his mouth and chewed.

* * *

Dad, Mum and Grandmother were waiting for me as I walked into the hotel lounge. Where was Uncle?

'Alex!' Mum cried. 'Did you get through?'

'Of course he got through, didn't you, Alex?' said Grandmother.

'I don't know how,' I said, 'but I did it! I got through!'

'And why are you so surprised? You know enough about cooking to win, son,' Dad said. 'We all know that, even if you don't.'

Mum hugged me and Dad looked very pleased. I was pretty pleased myself. I had got through to the finals without the help of my kung fu spice. I could hardly believe it!

'Hey, where's Uncle?' I asked. I couldn't see him anywhere.

'I'm sorry, Alex,' said Grandmother, 'but my brother told us he had to go back to the temple. It's just like him to disappear suddenly. He never changes! But he left this letter for you …'

Grandmother gave me an envelope. I opened it and inside was a letter and … the bag of kung fu spice! The letter said:

Dear Alex,

I have to go back to the Shaolin Temple. I have been asked to help a young man with his wu shu *– that's the real Chinese name for martial arts, which I also teach. Like you, he's good but he needs a little push.*

I knew you didn't need my help any more. I took the 'spice' out of your pocket while you weren't looking. It wasn't magic spice at all. It was just rice powder.

I'm sorry about my little lie. All you needed was confidence – not magic. I was right, wasn't I?

I will visit again next year. I want to taste more of your delicious cooking!

Tong Po

'So he *could* fight like Bruce Lee after all. I knew it!' said Mum as she read the letter. 'But what's all this about spice?'

'Just something I borrowed from Uncle,' I said. 'It's not important – not any more.'

I noticed Dad was smiling, but he had tears in his eyes. Mum had her arm round him.

'After all,' Dad said, 'you have a competition to win – right, son?'

I knew Dad was right. I knew I was good. I *could* win *Young Cook of the Year* now. Thanks to Uncle Tong Po I was a real kung fu cook.

With or without kung fu spice.

ACTIVITIES

1 Complete the sentences with the names in the box.

> Alex (x3)   Delia   Grandmother
> Great Uncle Tong Po (x2)

1 ....*Alex*............ works at weekends in his family's restaurant.
2 .... is not good at football.
3 .... lives in Hong Kong.
4 .... knows about Liverpool, not the rest of the country.
5 .... left home when he was very young.
6 .... takes the train from London to Liverpool.
7 .... enters a competition on TV.
8 .... leaves London suddenly.

2 Match the parts of the sentences.
1 Grandmother goes to Liverpool every February [c]
2 When Uncle comes to Liverpool, he [ ]
3 Uncle says that kung fu spice only works if you [ ]
4 Alex feels that with his kung fu spice he [ ]
5 At the London competition, Uncle knows that Alex [ ]
6 Alex discovers that the magic spice [ ]

a decides to teach Alex how to cook.
b can cook anything.
c to be with her family for Chinese New Year.
d doesn't need any more help.
e is just rice powder.
f cook with love.

3 Are the sentences true (*T*) of false (*F*)?

1 Grandmother has seen her brother recently. [F]
2 Uncle doesn't look like Alex expected him to look. ☐
3 Kung fu means 'a thing done well'. ☐
4 At first Alex thinks he can learn to cook as well as Uncle. ☐
5 Mum, Dad, Grandmother and Uncle go with Alex to the competition in Liverpool. ☐
6 Alex cooks Chinese food in the competition in London. ☐
7 At the competition Alex stays calm when he can't find the kung fu spice. ☐
8 Uncle is a martial arts teacher as well as a kung fu teacher. ☐

4 Answer the questions.

1 How is Alex feeling at the start of the story?

....

2 What does Grandmother complain about at the start of the story?

....

3 What does Uncle Tong Po teach Alex about cooking?

....

4 Why is Alex surprised to reach the final of the *Young Cook of the Year* competition?

....

....

Fugu

Time: the present
Place: a top Japanese restaurant in New York, USA

It was midnight. The restaurant was closed. The last customers had left and all the waiters had gone home.

Taro Yamada looked thoughtfully at his row of knives. They shone in the bright lights of the kitchen. He liked to tidy them away at the end of a long day.

The knives came in many sizes. They were all extremely sharp. Mr Yamada, after many years of practice, knew exactly how to use them. He had learned all about cutting fish when he was a young man. He used to work in the fish markets of Japan, where he cut up lots of fish every morning.

Taro had learned how to cook fish in Japan too. For many years he had worked in the finest fish restaurants in Japan. He had been the best chef in Tokyo. He could make the finest meals from all kinds of food from the oceans.

Yes, he had learned everything he needed to know. They had been good years. There was nobody who knew more about fish than Mr Taro Yamada. Nobody.

These days, Taro mainly prepared *sashimi* for customers in a Japanese restaurant in New York. *Sashimi* is finely-cut uncooked fish and it comes with a sauce. Taro could prepare *sashimi* really well. And the most expensive *sashimi* is *fugu*.

Fugu is the Japanese name for the puffer fish. Its skin, heart and liver[15] are all poisonous – although, sometimes, the liver is carefully prepared for people who want to try it. You can eat most other parts of the *fugu,* but it sometimes leaves a strange feeling in you. It is like feeling that you can't stand up or like having a strong alcoholic drink. The feeling comes from the very small amount of poison that is left in the fish.

Of course, if too much poison is left in the fish, it can kill you. *Fugu* must be prepared very, very carefully. If it isn't, you will die.

In fact, *fugu* is so dangerous that you have to be carefully trained and even have a special licence before you are allowed to prepare it.

Taro had the training and the licence. He was

the best. He knew just how to leave the right amount of poison in the *fugu* to suit every customer. He always looked carefully at the person who was going to eat it – like he was measuring somebody for a suit of clothes.

Taro himself didn't like *fugu*. He thought the taste was rather boring. But he knew that there were plenty of people who did enjoy it. Some people liked to eat it because it was dangerous. Some liked to show others that they could afford expensive food. Some ate it for both these reasons. It didn't matter what their reasons were. If they paid, Taro would prepare it for them.

It is said that the best *fugu* chefs can, if they want to, give a person enough poison so that they appear to die. The person *looks* dead, but they aren't really. And a few days later, they're all right again.

There were very few chefs in Tokyo who were clever enough, or even brave enough, to prepare *fugu* in this way.

Only this was not Tokyo. This was New York.

'Taro?'

It was Anzu, Taro's wife. She was always worried when she saw her husband in this thoughtful mood. Sometimes Taro looked at his sharp knives as if they could, in some way, cut him and Anzu free of all their worries. They had had plenty of those in the last four years.

'It's all right, Anzu,' Taro answered. 'Tell Iku I'll be out as soon as I've tidied this room a bit.'

Anzu nodded. She knew this was Taro's way of saying he wanted to be alone for a few minutes.

Their nephew, Iku, was the owner of the restaurant. Taro had left Tokyo four years ago and come to New York to become Iku's head chef. Iku had been a little surprised, but he had also been very pleased. Taro soon became known as the best Japanese chef in New York. And Iku's Place, which was the name of the restaurant, was a favourite of both Japanese and American people in New York. Business was good.

Iku didn't know the reason why Taro had left Tokyo. In fact, he knew very little about Taro. Nevertheless, he knew Taro was a good chef and that was enough for him.

Anzu liked her nephew. She didn't want him to worry about the reasons why she and Taro had left Tokyo. It was best that he didn't know.

When Anzu returned to the dining room, she saw Iku talking to two very large Japanese men dressed in smart suits. They were standing by the door. Even from where Anzu stood she noticed that the smaller of the two men had part of a finger missing.

She felt afraid.

'I'm sorry, sir,' Iku said again. 'As I said, we're closed. It's much too late for a meal. Please, come again tomorrow.'

Iku wasn't a small man. Difficult customers usually left when he asked them to. But these two men were even bigger than Iku. They looked very strong, too. They didn't move.

'We've come to see Taro Yamada,' said the man with half a finger. 'We've come a long way and we have a present for him.'

Anzu then noticed a large plastic box which the larger man was holding. It was like a suitcase, but more square. She didn't like the look of the 'present', even though she didn't know what it was. She knew the men and their box meant trouble. She had been expecting trouble ever since they had left Tokyo.

By now, Iku realised that these men were not going to go away.

'Look,' he said loudly, 'I'll call the police if I have to—'

'You don't have to, Iku,' Taro interrupted, as he walked into the dining room from the kitchen. 'I've been expecting these people for some time. Please let them in.'

'Are you sure, Uncle? I mean, look at the time ...'

'Please, Iku – I think it's best not to displease these gentlemen,' Taro said quietly. 'They've come a long way to see me. It would be very impolite if we turned them away.'

Taro paused. Iku could see his uncle look down at the box that the men were carrying. He looked at it too. And then he saw something in the shorter man's other hand – a gun!

Iku suddenly felt very afraid. He couldn't stop staring at the gun. And while he looked, he noticed a tattoo on the man's wrist. The picture belonged to the Yakuza, a Japanese society of criminals. These men were gangsters!

Half-Finger smiled.

'It's been a long time since we last met, Mr Yamada. My boss was very annoyed when you turned down his offer. It made him very unhappy. And then you disappeared. That was very rude of you.'

Iku, Taro and Anzu looked at one another.

'Offer?' Iku asked, despite his fear. 'What offer, Uncle? What do these men want?'

'Iku,' Taro began. 'In Tokyo people can make a lot of money from restaurants with the best chefs. These men wanted me to work for them in a restaurant of theirs. But I'm an honest man. I refused to work for gangsters. I left Tokyo because I didn't want to work for people like that.'

'But why did they want you, Uncle?' Iku asked. 'There are plenty of chefs in Tokyo!'

'We wanted Taro Yamada,' said Half-Finger, 'because he was the best *fugu* chef in the world. At least, that's what my boss said. My boss thinks *fugu* is the greatest Japanese food of all. He says Taro Yamada's *fugu* is the best. "I want Taro Yamada," he says and what my boss wants he gets!'

Taro noticed Half-Finger touch the part of his finger that was left as he spoke. He knew that gangsters in the Yakuza had to cut off a finger if they made a mistake or displeased their boss. Half-Finger had to please his boss before he lost another finger – or maybe his life.

'Now,' Half-Finger said quietly, 'you make *fugu* for us and we'll see just how good you are.'

'We don't do real *fugu*,' said Anzu. 'We're not allowed to prepare it here – it's too dangerous because of the poison. And we can't get fresh *fugu* puffer fish here. We have to get them sent to us from Japan.'

'We know that,' Half-Finger said. He made a sign to the bigger man, who then put the plastic box on a table.

'Our present – fresh *fugu* puffer fish, still alive. Two of them. These are *tora-fugu* – the best *fugu* of all.'

The big man opened the plastic box. It contained, in water, two *tora-fugu* and they were still very much alive. *Tora-fugu* are considered to be the most poisonous of all the different kinds of *fugu*. They are also the most valuable. The lips[18] of the two fish, Taro noticed, had been sewn closed to stop them biting each other. These men knew what they were doing.

'And if I don't want to make *fugu* for you?' Taro asked.

'You have already been rude to us when you refused our first offer,' said Half-Finger. 'To refuse us again would not be acceptable. I think you understand me. I think all of you do, eh?'

Taro knew. Iku and Anzu knew too. If Taro refused to prepare the fish, these men would kill them all.

'And if I do it, what then?' Taro asked.

'Then you work for us in Tokyo,' Half-Finger replied. 'My boss wants you as his own private chef. Of course, your wife will come too. Your nephew,' he pointed to Iku, 'can stay here. I'm sure he can find another chef for his restaurant. And I'm sure he can keep his mouth shut.'

'Our boss wants us to watch you prepare the *fugu* and then eat some ourselves,' said the other man. 'You were once the best. Are you still the best? Or have you forgotten how to prepare *tora-fugu*? We'll soon find out. If you're not good enough, we'll kill you anyway, so don't try anything stupid.'

Taro knew he had no choice. He had to prepare *fugu* for these men.

* * *

In the kitchen Half-Finger watched Taro prepare the fish while the other man watched Anzu and Iku prepare the vegetables. The men's guns were pointing at them all the time.

Even Half-Finger could see how good Taro was as he watched him at work. Taro used a special small knife to cut open the *fugu* while they were still alive. He quickly cut away the parts people didn't eat, putting the liver – which was the most expensive part – to one side. Then he cut the fish into very thin pieces and arranged it on two plates with the vegetables, rice and special sauce.

The Yakuza men watched every move.

'It's all ready,' Taro said, as he put the plates onto a table in the dining area. 'Please. Sit down and enjoy your meal.'

Half-Finger smiled. 'It looks good. But I am a polite man. I cannot be the first to eat. After you, Mr Yamada. The liver first.'

Taro looked nervous. 'But I thought you wanted to try it yourself?'

'And I will,' said Half-Finger, 'after I've seen you eat it. We're not stupid – you could have left enough poison in it to kill us. So if you thought you could get rid of us, forget it – you'll be the one to die. Now eat!'

Taro's face was sweating as he picked up a small piece of *fugu* liver with his chopsticks. He raised it to his mouth slowly.

'Taro! No!' cried Anzu. 'Let me eat it first!'

Taro looked at his wife. There were tears in his eyes. He shook his head.

'No, they want me to eat this, so I must eat.'

Taro placed the food into his mouth. He chewed and then swallowed.[16] He had eaten the *fugu*. He shut his eyes and opened them again. Nothing happened. The two big men looked as though they had hoped something would happen.

'I've heard the poison works quite slowly,' said Half-Finger. 'Let's wait a bit longer.'

So they waited and watched as Taro sat quietly eating some vegetables. They watched him for ten minutes, maybe longer.

Then suddenly, Taro started breathing quickly. He put his hands to his throat and fell to the floor. His body shook violently for a few seconds and then he lay still.

Anzu was silent, her eyes open wide.

Iku cried, 'He's dead! You've killed him!'

Half-Finger laughed. 'If he's dead, he's killed himself. But I want to make sure first!'

He nodded to the other gangster. The big man bent down and looked closely at Taro's eyes. He turned to Half-Finger and nodded.

'The old man is dead,' said Half-Finger. 'My friend has seen enough dead guys to know that. No need to waste any more of our time. He's useless to us now. We'll tell our boss that his chef wasn't as good as he thought he was.'

Both of the Yakuza men laughed. Half-Finger touched his short finger again. He was hoping his boss would agree with him.

Iku felt his mouth go dry. He looked at Taro as he lay on the floor and tears started falling from his eyes. Anzu began crying loudly as she bent over the still body of her husband.

'We're going now. Please don't call the police or tell anyone about this meeting. Or there will be problems for you and your families. Do you understand?'

Iku nodded.

The two men left and shut the door.

A few moments passed and then Iku asked, 'Should I call the police, Auntie?'

Anzu lifted up her head and, to Iku's surprise, she was smiling.

'No, Iku. We've got rid of them at last. Now help me carry Taro to a bed. Then we'll call the hospital and wait.'

'Wait?' Iku cried. 'What do you mean?'

'I know my husband very well,' Anzu said. 'He knew exactly what he was doing. Taro is still the best – the very best. We wait …'

ACTIVITIES

1 **Put the sentences in order.**

1 Taro feels ill. ☐
2 Taro gets a special 'present'. ☐
3 Taro goes to work at Iku's restaurant in New York. ☐
4 Taro has to prepare a dangerous meal. ☐
5 Taro learns to cut fish in the fish markets of Japan. ☐1☐
6 Taro was a top chef in Tokyo. ☐
7 The two gangsters think that Taro is dead. ☐
8 Two Japanese men arrive at Iku's Place looking for Taro. ☐

2 **Are the sentences true (*T*) of false (*F*)?**

1 *Sashimi* is fish which is cooked in a special sauce. ☐F☐
2 A small amount of *fugu* poison won't kill you. ☐
3 *Fugu* is Taro's favourite fish. ☐
4 Iku's restaurant is only popular with Japanese people. ☐
5 Taro was expecting the gangsters to find him. ☐
6 When Iku sees the gun, he realises the gangsters are Yakusa criminals. ☐
7 Taro refused the gangster's job offer in Tokyo. ☐
8 Iku's place can sell real *fugu*. ☐
9 Taro, Iku and Anzu will die unless Taro makes *fugu* for the gangsters. ☐
10 At the end of the story, Anzu thinks that Taro is dead. ☐

80

3 Read the sentences from the text and answer the questions.

1 Iku had been a little surprised, but he had also been very pleased. (page 72)
Why do you think Iku feels like this?

2 'And I'm sure he can keep his mouth shut.' (page 76)
What does Half-Finger mean when he says this?

3 The two big men looked as though they had hoped something would happen. (page 78)
What did the gangsters expect would happen?

4 'He knew exactly what he was doing.' (page 79)
What does Anzu mean when she says this at the end of the story?

4 Answer the questions.

1 Why do people eat *fugu*?

2 Why didn't Taro accept the job offer in Tokyo?

3 Why did one of the gangsters have only half a finger?

4 Why did the gangsters make Taro eat the *fugu* before they tried it?

5 Do you think that Taro dies from eating the *fugu*? Why / Why not?

Changes

Time: the present
Place: Sheffield, England

Everybody knew about the comet. It was in all the newspapers. When it finally passed close to the Earth, it lit up the sky for three nights. It was beautiful. People who were not usually interested in looking beyond their television screens took at least one look outside.

Even people like Darren.

Darren was looking in the bathroom mirror at the spots on his face. They were near his nose. His mum always said he got spots because he ate too many sweets. But he hated sweets. And he never ate chocolate. His mum *loved* chocolate and *she* never got spots. It wasn't fair. Darren was just going to examine his biggest spot when his mum called out.

'Darren! Darren, look at this!'

'Aw, Mum. I'm busy!'

But Darren's mum refused to take no for an answer. She knew her thirteen-year-old son liked science fiction. A bit of science fact would do him no harm. This sort of thing didn't happen every day, after all. They said that this comet was only going to pass the Earth once. She didn't want Darren to miss it.

'Darren Miller, come down right now!'

When Darren got downstairs, the door to the garden was open. He could see both his parents outside. They were looking up, their faces lit by a gentle light. He went out and stood next to them. Then he, too, looked up.

It was, indeed, a lovely thing to see. Darren was pleased his mum had called him. The sky was full of beautiful, coloured light. It made Darren think of Christmas lights and all the bright colours he loved when he was younger.

It was so beautiful that he almost forgot about his spots.

*   *   *

The next day all of the newspapers were full of pictures and stories about the comet. Some of the newspapers were quite excited about it, because the comet had passed very close to the Earth.

'Comet nearly hits Earth!' said one headline in a newspaper.

'Earth escapes comet!' said another.

Most of the newspaper reports also mentioned the beauty of the comet. They all said how lucky we were to see such a wonderful thing.

Of course, there were the usual pessimists who said that the comet would put something nasty into the air we breathe. Others said the comet was a sign that the end of the Earth was coming. However, most people took no notice of these warnings.

Life went on as usual.

Life for Darren meant getting ready for school again after the holidays. Comets were nice but now he had more important things to think about. He had to make himself look good for the beautiful Vanessa.

Darren's school was just an ordinary school in the city of Sheffield in England. It was no better than any other school in Sheffield.

But it *did* have Vanessa.

Vanessa was a brown-haired, brown-eyed girl in the same year as Darren. She had smiled at Darren once. He remembered it well. It had happened in the last week before the holidays. He had let her go in front of him in the queue for lunch. She hadn't said 'thank you,' but she had given him a little smile. It had showed her perfect white teeth.

He had been too nervous to speak to her. He just couldn't do it. It would be easier, he felt, to grow wings and fly up to the ceiling.

This time he would be ready. He would put on lots of deodorant to make himself smell nice. He wanted to have another look at his spots and, just maybe, have a shave. The night before he had felt something above his mouth that might be the first hairs of a moustache.

He made sure he got to the bathroom before everyone else that morning. He wanted to have a close look at those spots … and his new moustache.

'Darren, will you be in there for a long time?' It was Darren's mum. 'Your father wants to use the bathroom.'

Darren knew his dad always spent ages in the bathroom. Well, his dad could wait today, for a change.

'I'll be out soon, Mum,' said Darren.

But he was lying. He wanted to look good and smell good. It could take a long time. His new deodorant smelled very good this morning. He suddenly noticed all the different smells that went into it. There were flowers, spices – lots of things he had never smelled before. His nose felt a bit wet too. Was he getting a cold? Probably not, if he could smell things so well.

Darren walked over to the mirror and looked at his face. His face looked worse than ever!

His nose was wet and shiny. It was moving a lot, like an animal's nose. It looked like a rabbit smelling its breakfast. But this wasn't the most shocking thing. His top lip had long, thick hairs on it. They were like the hairs on an animal's nose. They were like the whiskers of a rabbit!

Darren screamed.

*   *   *

Time: *the present*
Place: *Singapore*

Julie Ong had been fourteen for three weeks. A lot of her friends were fourteen too. They all agreed that a young woman should watch her weight. It was especially important not to eat sweets and cakes. Julie hadn't eaten a cake or a piece of chocolate since her birthday. But there were still no signs that her parents saw Julie as a young woman. To them, she was still a child.

Then there was the strange thing with the comet. Everybody was talking about it. Julie's English teacher gave her class homework about it. They had to describe the comet in a poem. It was so unfair! The comet had been quite beautiful, but writing about it was no fun at all. Julie decided to take a break from her Sunday morning homework. Instead of writing she would comb her long black hair in the mirror. It was more interesting than writing a poem, at least.

Her parents wouldn't notice that she was wasting time. She could hear them at the other end of the house talking about the comet. They weren't talking loudly, but she could still hear them. Her hearing wasn't normally that good. It was very odd.

Julie picked up her hairbrush – her favourite pink one – and walked towards her bedroom mirror. But when she looked at herself, she immediately noticed something strange. There were two things rising up and out from her hair. They were on both sides of her head. Julie pushed back her hair and saw that the two things were her ears. They were now pointed at the top, like an animal's ears, and they were bigger too. Much bigger.

Julie fainted.[17]

* * *

Darren's new whiskers grew even longer over the next week. His nose became much, much better at smelling things too. He could smell almost anything from a long distance away now. His dad had his own smell, so had his mum. Everybody had their own smell.

Having a good nose was useful and Darren liked it. He liked his whiskers too, and he couldn't really shave them off. It would hurt, he was sure, if he tried. Anyway, he was getting used to them.

In Singapore, Julie Ong discovered that her hearing had become extremely good. She could hear almost everything.

Darren didn't know it yet, but the beautiful Vanessa had now grown long teeth like a cat's. She had whiskers too. And suddenly she seemed to enjoy eating a lot of fish.

Darren, Julie and Vanessa were not alone.

Sudden changes were happening all over the world. Many young people between the ages of twelve and eighteen had developed the special strength of some kind of animal. Sometimes it wasn't immediately obvious – like having the fantastic eyesight of a hunting bird. But often the changes were obvious. Some had grown long tails and they could hold on to things with them. Some had webbed skin on their hands and feet so that they could swim fast. Some had the strength of a bull; others could run as fast as a horse. They all looked human still, but in some way they had changed.

Of course, adults everywhere were extremely worried. Why had their children changed? What had produced the changes? What could they do to help their children?

* * *

Darren discovered that his amazing nose had many advantages too. He found that he could tell what mood people were in just by their smell – even if they were trying to hide it. That was useful.

This new sense of smell was useful in other ways too. If he lost something, he could always find it by using his nose. He helped his mum buy the freshest and tastiest food in the supermarket.

He now used deodorant which didn't have a strong smell. His new nose didn't like strong smells any more.

'You'd better not get too used to it,' said his dad. 'Some day soon we'll be able to get you back the way you were.'

'Maybe, Dad,' Darren said. 'But what if I don't want to go back to the way I was?'

Darren's father didn't say anything. Like many other parents, he didn't understand how his son could like the changes. He wanted the old Darren back – the Darren without the whiskers and the amazing sense of smell.

And *why* had some young people changed while others hadn't? That was the question every adult in the world was asking.

* * *

Some adults blamed the children themselves for the changes. They said they watched too much TV or ate the wrong things or didn't behave in the right way.

Most people blamed the comet.

'Comet causes horrible teenage changes!' was the kind of headline found on the front page of many newspapers. They all had similar stories. Everybody was saying that it must have been the comet – what else could it have been? The comet had, in some strange way, affected the bodies of some teenagers.

'I don't think the changes are horrible!' said Julie to her friends. 'I think my new hearing is very useful. I think my ears are rather beautiful too!'

Some of Julie's friends agreed with her.

'I like my new wings,' said one.

'I can change colour like a chameleon[21] – isn't that cool?' said another.

Teenagers everywhere were comparing their changes.

Some were stronger, others were faster, others could jump higher. But no matter what changes happened, they were still teenagers.

But then something strange happened. Some teenagers began to return to normal. Some eventually lost all sign of their changes and went back to what they had been before.

But *why*?

The answer came almost by accident.

A teen called Danny was given a job in an advertisement. Danny had wings and he could fly. In the advertisement, Danny had to fly over a children's party and give out chocolate biscuits. Danny hated chocolate biscuits, but he had to eat some during the advertisement. It was after he ate his second biscuit that something started happening. His wings started to get smaller. Soon they disappeared completely. He couldn't fly any more. Danny was a 'normal' teenager again. Why had it happened?

It was the chocolate. It had to be.

Scientists tested the effect of chocolate on other teenagers. They discovered that if the teenagers ate a few things with chocolate in them, they went back to normal. The world now knew why some children hadn't been affected by the comet. The mystery was solved.[20]

The comet had only changed teenagers who didn't eat chocolate!

* * *

'I don't like chocolate, you know that,' Darren told his parents. 'I've never liked it.'

'But all you have to do is eat a bit and you'll go back to normal!' said Dad. 'You want to be normal again, don't you, Darren?'

Darren thought about Vanessa. He liked her new cat looks. Vanessa had found Darren's changes attractive too. She had spoken to him quite a lot lately.

'If you mean do I want to be like most of my friends, then yes. But some of my friends have changed and we like the changes. Why should I want to go back? Anyway, I hate chocolate.'

His parents couldn't make him change his mind. Maybe if his friends agreed to change back, Darren would too.

But that wasn't as easy as it seemed. A lot of teenagers felt the same way as Darren.

* * *

Some adults accepted their new teenagers because the changes were useful in daily life. If you were faster and stronger, for example, you could work better.

But most adults expected that their teenagers would want to return to how they had been before.

Many of them did.

But a lot of teenagers simply didn't care what the adults wanted. They refused to eat the chocolate.

* * *

In Singapore, Julie Ong finally ate some chocolate. Soon, her beautiful big ears were gone. She often remembered them and was sad.

In Sheffield, Darren Miller was using his nose to enjoy the sweet smell of the carrots growing in Vanessa's garden. Vanessa watched him happily as she ate a fish on top of the garden wall.

ACTIVITIES

●●●●●●●●●●●●●●●●●●●●●●●●●●●●●●●●●●●●●●●

1 Complete the sentences with the names in the box.

> Danny (x2)   Darren (x3)   Julie   Vanessa (x2)

1 _Darren_ has a problem with spots.
2 _____ is a girl who is at the same school as Darren.
3 _____ discovers that he looks like a rabbit.
4 _____ discovers that she's got big, pointed ears.
5 _____ discovers that she looks like a cat.
6 _____ has wings and can fly.
7 _____ has to eat chocolate biscuits.
8 _____ tells his parents that he is happy with himself as he is now.

2 <u>Underline</u> the correct words in each sentence.
1 The comet filled the sky with light for *a night / three nights*.
2 Darren *eats lots of / never eats* sweets and chocolate.
3 Darren wants to look good for *his parents / Vanessa*.
4 When Darren first sees the changes to his face, he *screams / smiles*.
5 Julie realises that she can *see / hear* much better than before.
6 Scientists discovered that the comet had only changed young people who *ate / didn't eat* chocolate.
7 A lot of young people who have changed *want / don't want* to change back to how they were.

3 What do the underlined words refer to in these lines from the text?

1 She didn't want Darren to miss <u>it</u>. (page 82)

The comet

2 <u>It</u> was moving a lot, like an animal's nose. (page 85)

3 <u>It</u> was very odd. (page 86)

4 Why had <u>it</u> happened? (page 91)

5 'But all you have to do is eat <u>a bit</u> and you'll go back to normal!' said Dad.

6 She often remembered <u>them</u> and was sad. (page 93)

4 Answer the questions.

1 Why does Darren's mother want him to see the comet?

2 What do pessimistic people say about the comet?

3 Why didn't Julie eat cakes or chocolate after her fourteenth birthday?

4 How is Darren's new sense of smell useful to him and his family?

5 Why do some parents accept the changes to their children?

LOOKING BACK

5 Check your answers to *Before you read* on page 3.

Glossary

[1]**ignore** (page 8) *verb*   to not give attention to something or someone

[2]**invention** (page 8) *noun*   something that has been designed or made for the first time

[3]**appetite** (page 10) *noun*   the feeling that makes you want to eat

[4]**product** (page 11) *noun*   something that someone makes or grows so that they can sell it

[5]**pie** (page 12) *noun*   a kind of food made with fruit, vegetables or meat which is covered in pastry and baked

[6]**research** (page 13) *noun*   when someone studies a subject in order to discover more information about it

[7]**herb** (page 26) *noun*   a plant whose leaves are used in cooking to add flavour to food

[8]**temple** (page 33) *noun*   a building where people in some religions go to pray

[9]**emperor** (page 34) *noun*   the male ruler of an empire

[10]**referee** (page 41) *noun*   someone who makes sure that players follow the rules during a sports game

[11]**tradition** (page 51) *noun*   a custom or way of behaving that has continued for a long time in a group of people

[12]**priest** (page 53) *noun*   someone who performs religious duties and ceremonies

[13]**beat** (page 63) *verb*   to defeat someone in a competition

[14]**judge** (page 63) *verb*   to decide the winner or results of a competition

[15]**liver** (page 71) *noun*   a part in your body that cleans your blood

[16]**swallow** (page 78) *verb*   to move your throat in order to make food or drink go down

[17]**faint** (page 86) *verb*   to suddenly become unconscious for a short time, usually falling down

[18]**solve** (page 91) *verb*   to find the answer to something